LET ME
REASSURE
YOU

Other books by Arlene Graston

SPECIAL FRIENDS
Tales of Saints and Animals

THUMBELINA
Tale by Hans Christian Andersen
Translation by Erik Haugaard

IN EVERY MOON THERE IS A FACE
Poem by Charles Mathes

DO YOU REMEMBER?
Whispers from a Spiritual World

THE CHILDREN'S PROMISE
A Visit to a Spiritual Garden

Remembering
Reality

LET ME
REASSURE
YOU

Written and Illustrated by
ARLENE GRASTON

ISBN 978-0-9848814-6-8

Book design by Arlene Graston and Drew Stevens

VISIBLES, INC
New York

I must not lose sight of You, I said,

as I entered the dream.

But I did.

"For once you have tasted flight
you will walk the earth with your eyes
turned skywards, for there you have been
and there you will long to return."
LEONARDO DA VINCI

"All true Knowledge originates out
of our inner self, in quiet communication
with our soul. Doctrines and civilizations have
exploited us from our stillness, have taken away
from us this knowledge. We know everything
deep within ourselves. We were made to
believe that we need to be instructed, and
our own spiritual self was suppressed."
EDWARD BACH

"O God, I could be bounded in a nutshell
and count myself a king of infinite space,
were it not that I have bad dreams."
SHAKESPEARE
(*Hamlet*: Act 2, Scene 2)

Dear fellow traveler. . .

I am not an exceptional person. I am simply someone whose earliest memories are from before birth. I brought with me the consciousness of the unlimited Life and spent my childhood making myself turn away from its reality in order to fit into a limited, sensual world. This decision enabled me to experience a world similar to everyone else but with the deep regret of knowing I am not being myself.

The spirit of Wholeness permeates my work as an artist and writer and it is not letting me forget that the perception I once put away has remained in me wanting to be expressed. My writing forms the gentle narrative I long to hear. I originally created this book for myself, to lovingly assemble the heartening assurances of the deep-feeling qualities of the one true life. I hope my telling a bit of my story and sharing insights from my spiritual self will be meaningful and inspiring to you.

In gentle companionship,
Arlene Graston

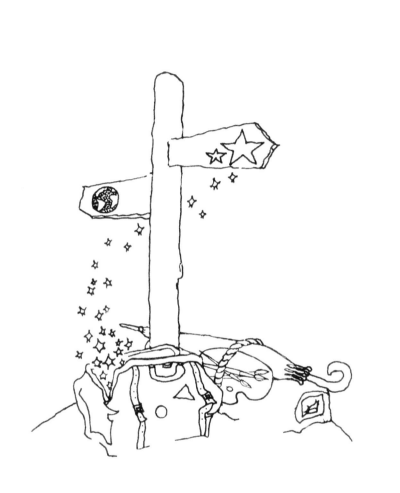

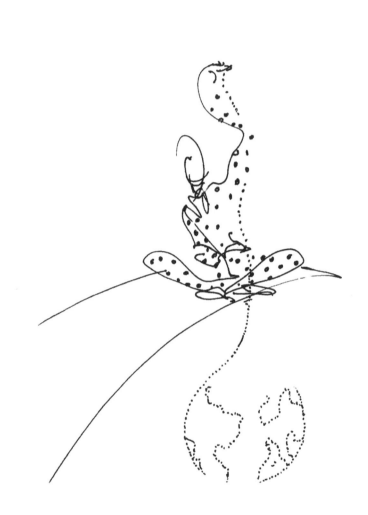

CONTENTS

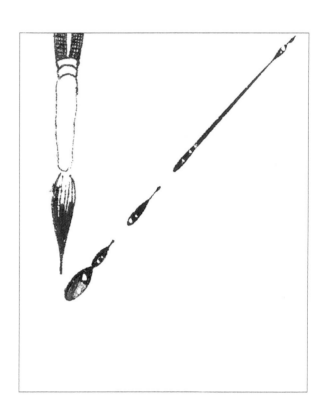

THROUGH THE INVISIBLE DOOR

The cover of this book depicts a little girl as she stands looking to the stars. She looks there to find what is true. She knows she is more than a girl and that stars are not far-away things with no connection to her. But now she is alone in a dream where reality is outside herself and nothing is what it seems. She has become lost.

I was that little girl. I had the awareness of the warm, supportive way of existence before birth. I knew myself to be in right relationship with life, one with all living things. Then I joined a world that believed in good and bad, right and wrong where I became an objectified separateness called a human being.

There was a small door on the left side of the room as you looked at that far wall. It could not be seen later in the day—once closed it disappeared from view. Each morning I walked through that door coming from a world bathed in Light. Behind the door was a little stairway. I made my way down gradually appearing plain wooden steps to enter a room and to become the little girl lying on the blue bed waiting to walk me through her world. Each night as the child slept I left her body and returned to the other side of the invisible door.

Dream? At breakfast, when they'd speak of dreams they'd had in the night, I'd say, "Oh, no, *this* is the dream, and do we have to go on meeting like this?" I was starting to identify with being the child when I was in her body and I quickly became weary of this constraint. It seems they never heard me because they never answered.

I began this journey with an open heart and was optimistic that I could hold onto my Light and share its reality. This was something I profoundly

wanted to do. I remember planning the trip: I remember standing as if at a window, looking onto
a scene below and being excited that I would
soon be within it. I saw land near water; I heard
the most engaging music. (I've been hooked on
jazz ever since I got here. And I live on an island.)

I knew that the players I'd meet were waiting
where the most cultured and materialistic world-
view replaced inner-knowing. My mother had a
dream while pregnant with me where I appeared
to her as the adult me; my grandfather knew I
was coming without being told, announcing the
precise date of my birth. Before we met, my future husband would hang on the wall of his office
prints of the cathedral of Reims, my birthplace.
For my work as an artist, I was born with a tiny
callous on the middle finger of my right hand
which grew as I grew; it cushions my pencils and
brushes perfectly. I had all my breadcrumbs in
place.

At the physical birth I was thrilled to be entering

this world. What a Big Adventure! I rolled up my sleeves and grabbed my kit bag. I felt the eager anticipation that I feel today when I start something new.

What I entered into was a strident environment of seemingly solid images and assaulting noise—most of it created by *unspoken* thoughts forming a mute cacophony. It was a world still reeling from a war and a family recovering from the loss of a son and brother. The sense of possibilities was remote and the mood was one of suppressed despair—so contrary to the lighthearted and supportive environment I was coming from.

But babies bring hope for the future and I was welcomed. Even though they believed in the worldly concept of blood-ties, no one was conventional enough to impose, consciously or subconsciously, many social expectations onto me. My soul remained expanded and this allowed me to begin my time here fully awake. However, it was a long while before I consented to enter the body "full time." When I did, I found it frustrating to be tuned to only one channel. And it was confusing to find myself beginning to think and act in the ways of a human child. A role-playing personality was taking over!

No one is a stranger in Spirit but I found myself a stranger now. Imagine my confusion when I could not refer to where I had just come from because no one seemed to know that they had come from there, too. Even my mother and grandfather, who had been expecting me, were under a spell. I was in a make-believe realm where the inhabitants were unconscious of the vibrant inner life in the individual. They had replaced it with reliance on inert external symbols and facts and aggressively enforced this point of view on one another.

School was insanity for me. It was a place that specialized in the denial of the individual's absolute direct knowing. I hated every single minute in the place. Trapped in a body, shut up in a room, I was learning to be obedient and never to question lifeless materialistic assumptions. Apparently children were thought to be empty mechanical creatures with no original discernment and knowledge of their own. They needed to be taught everything . . . about everything. The point was to absorb and regurgitate. No thought was given to life being complete. No one was using Imagination to create "out of thin air" the thing wanted from the infinite source always at hand. Only what presently existed on the planet or had been previously thought and recorded was to be taken into account. This systematic conditioning produced a "superior intellect" that righteously dismissed the ways of Intuition. Beautiful free beings were turned into fixed entities, categorized and typecast into mere concepts of themselves.

Reality as I knew it was being re-interpreted, freeze-dried, and thrown at me in a book report.

Life (Life!) reduced to a scientific *explanation*, a merely observable thing made for measuring, not for being lived spontaneously with empowered dignity, to say nothing of joy. All this incomprehensibleness came at me with such *conviction* that it was hard to look away. Dumbfounding as it was, in this human quality alone I found their feeling-being. I couldn't help but respond and pay respectful attention to *any* genuineness I found. To my dismay, the inner feeling-self was never alluded to. Not theirs. Not mine. Not ever. Superficiality ruled the day and Originality died an unobserved death. I sat there and watched how a false sense of life and its resulting insecurity was inculcated into vulnerable minds. I was in a very bad dream. I realized I was the only one who saw it that way when I asked how did all this "learning" help one to be happy and to experience happiness. You can guess the results. I felt my little wings close.

The innocent child I was said things that did not go over well. I learned to keep them to myself and eventually *from* myself. In secret I did many things in defiance of the laws of physics, abilities that I lost one by one. Being able to walk through walls and fly over stairs is natural when you don't know it's an odd thing to do (although I instinctively never did such things in front of others). I stopped being able to do these things when I became conscious I was doing them.

I vigilantly scrutinized the ways of the cultures I found myself in. Each one had a different set of rules and none acknowledged the deeper feeling life. All civilizations are incomplete, but I believe primitive cultures are truer to the nature of reality than the materialistic cultures I have lived in.

Life is *creative*. The Western world is proud of its ability to create all that "stuff out there." It even glorifies itself for thinking materialistically. We are always using the ways of Infinite Mind and its ideas and principles since there is only *one* reality. But dreaming *through a glass darkly, we* distort its truth and perceive a manifest universe disconnected from us. We are "born" into an atmosphere that seems to "make its purpose" to condition us to see separateness and limitation. This does make for a very interesting world and would not be such a problem if we weren't all *suffering from being full of fear; and acting crazy*. Might that be a clue? Unhappiness is just not "normal" in Spirit.

And so, my personal energy-field was contracting as I identified more and more with a body. I was falling under the spell myself—having to censor myself was robbing me of unlimited awareness and self-authority. The empowering inner Presence was fading and my interior self became the world of "other people" and their perception of things. The linear fiction of this world became my life and I did all I could to adapt. Not only was

I a stranger in this world, I was now a stranger to myself saying things and acting in ways unlike anything true to my nature.

Yet I "loved people most of all in this world," I wrote in my very first essay my second year at school. And I did, but they were so "earth-bound," so locked in the dream. They really believed the parts they were playing. There was no reaching them. That's why I felt at home in train stations as a child. They were the one place where people were playing a "role" that was authentic. Suitcase in hand, they became my unacknowledged fellow travelers and I would stop feeling so alone for a while. (When I grew up I was going to have a magazine kiosk in a train station to always be in a nearly truthful place!)

Ultimately my strategy was simply to please everybody rather than myself—particularly since they kept calling me selfish and stubborn when I dared to not share their point of view. I found so many "never-questioned" notions to question, what was the point of arguing? It was all so hopeless.

To suddenly be confronted with gravity is pretty disorienting, but it was the fear of taking action in the world because of the social interdiction against expressing things truthfully that caused a dramatic split from my sense of self. I was eight and was told in class that we could paint anything we wanted. Naturally, I was going to paint "God." When I remembered that the nature of "God" was something people didn't perceive I painted a church, something they could see. In that small compromise my wings closed tighter.

It was the day I concluded that I must no longer apply the "inside" ways, that I lost my mooring. Those ways were not in use here and this single decision, to use only the external time-dependent methods of this world altered my nature forever. I began second-guessing myself about everything;

never sure what was the right thing to do. Life became, "when in Rome . . ." My childhood was a learned disavowal of the internal life. I became a displaced person.

I was lost. Where was the Light that imbued me with Infinite knowledge and abilities? Why did I have to give up my free, happy self that spanned the planes of Foreverness with expansive wings of wonder? And, honestly, what *was* this arrogant world, steeped in ridiculously delusional thinking? Why did I have to become like it?

But the *heartbreaking* aspect of my new existence had to do with losing my *very good relationship with life*. Where was it? I'd been unselfconsciously sharing reality peaceably with all living beings. Suddenly I was an outsider in the universe, always wrong about everything, and having to alter my behavior so as to not get anybody mad at me.

Of course I fully understand now that it was my

acquiescence to all this that became my downfall and left me wondering how to stay sane in duality. How could I love people without letting them drive me crazy?

It's ironic that outwardly none of my inner confusion showed. I was a cheerful child with funny impish ways. I was affectionate and ready to share with others. Although I was extremely sensitive and easily hurt, I had a sense of humor and plenty of common sense. I presented myself with a smiling face, always an agreeable little helper—the classic "good little girl." In time as I got to know the world, I became less social and more circumspect. I was unaware that I stopped wanting anything for myself, or even that I *could* want anything for myself.

But I knew I did want to *survive*. Thankfully I still had the memory of a deeper reality so I saw through the conventions and the conditional thinking. This enabled me to sense and avoid many potential pitfalls and to create opportunities. The first thing I did was make an early escape from school. I knew it was possible to teach myself anything I needed to know and to make something brand new and original happen without needing a precedent for it. I taught myself commercial design skills. This resulted in a career, on two continents that allowed for a rather charmed life and paid all the bills. I was enjoying this material world on one hand, but I kept resisting its unrelenting and soul-stultifying materialism on the other.

The *"something* missing" was still missing. A nameless emptiness would regularly paralyze me in the despair and depression that I kept hidden from my friends. There was no way to talk about the other reality I missed, even to myself. I gave up.

And then, unexpectedly, I found an answer to this emptiness. Not an "and-now-the-problem-is-solved-forever" kind of answer, but an on-going discourse to my silent questioning. And it came from *me*!

When I stopped using my talents for commercial gain, I began painting images that revealed a wondrously joyful world. A world I knew and loved. And when I started writing, I surprised myself by hearing in the written words a voice reassuring and familiar. It acknowledged my unusual human experience and addressed the sadness and loss I'd been carrying in my heart. I soon realized I was hearing from my "lost" Self. It was news from Home.

I found I wasn't receiving *rules* for how to live my human life; instead, I was getting persistent, gentle reminders of the true nature of my being. *Trust yourself*—something was saying. *Let go the world.* Thinking ourselves human is the very belief that removes us from the reality of Spirit. The only way to deal with misperception is to "break the frame"—to look through the appearance. In reading my writing I was rediscovering Spirit's subtle ways and regaining faith in my uncomplicated self.

My writing is simple and kind and very very encouraging. It tells me I didn't have to give up anything. It urges me to identify with being Spirit and to forego the human attitudes and beliefs that have prevented my self-expression. It reminds me that I am whole, that my mind and my life do not need to be added to.

Most important to me, it reassures me that I have kept my loving heart despite my too frequent irritation and impatience with the ways of this world. My writing breaks the spell of that world by not sounding like it. It doesn't speak through a doctrine or tradition. Its nature is abstract; being

Soul it is *lyrical* and unconcerned with material minutiae even though it is the Source that forms human experience. I am reminded that Heart, the innerness of being, is what matters, not how brilliantly I contribute to The Culture. Social sophistication, so valued in my environment, is a glamorous diversion from the inner reality—our inner self has no allegiance to an external order. It just guides us through it.

Quiet poetic language, more than meditation, makes me *feel* that I am part of a sustaining simplicity. I now see *why* and *how* I gave up my true self in order to live here peacefully. Ultimately there was practical wisdom in my "capitulating to the movie." I am all for peace. This insight enables me to understand, let go, and move on. And I am learning what being Selfish really means—a word much used to control us. I am seeing that what is missing in this world is the genuine valuing of *self*. After all, "self" is Universal Love individualized. Self, in materialism, is confused with the world-conditioned personality sense of being. That explains a "look at me!" culture. True self-acceptance is the essential quality of harmonious behavior with all life. We have been *taught* to doubt ourselves. In a world of people feeling insecure, mind-games take place.

I feel I may be reaching the clearing in the forest of my great adventure. To have lost a joyful, expansive nature by placing myself in a small restrictive box where thoughts full of shadows and fears create the world . . . well, I have no words for how truly disconcerting that is. I do know it takes courage to go through it, for *everyone*. But the struggle becomes a blessing when making the way back from what merely *feels* so real, to what *is* so thankfully true. At a human level everything I went through had a reason for being but I know I don't need to analyze or understand it—I need only to be in the present. The real challenge has been to stay awake in the midst of the Strange Great Urge that descends upon us to fall asleep and forget who we are. This ancient troublemaker has been portrayed as the magic spell in our fairy-tales. It is that.

I am shy about sharing my spiritual story. How to speak about the Ineffable? Yet we're all in a dream and need perspective. I believe that in silencing our hard-edged intellect (which we think is who we are) and filling our hearts with soft loving words that describe our higher nature, we re-awaken our awareness of that nature. And, when we find *our own meaningful words and say them*, we are made whole. After all, it was constantly considering the world's hard-edged concepts that caused us to lose sight of our inner reality. We become what we contemplate. What will that be?

All my life my inner being has stood poised near the "invisible door". . . waiting. In the end it was my *playful expression* as a writer and an artist that brought me the beauty and the assurance of the presence of the Heart that lives behind that door and *in all of us.* Words from this Universal Heart are worth sharing. Who knows when and how an Invisible Door will open. ❖ ❖

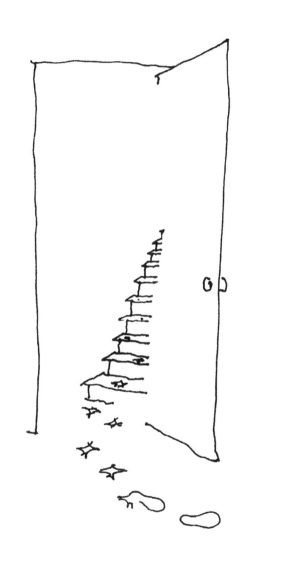

ONE

LOOKING FOR THE DOOR

 It seems funny to you to be expressing yourself with the help of backlit keys like these. Sparkling keys suit you, what you find in using them is your very Soul itself. Within the illuminating map that is every word you write, is a whisper from the "first self" you were—the one who calmly walked through a hint of a door each morning to enter time from timelessness.

The door became invisible because you grew to believe that you were to turn away from the truth beyond it.

Loss is an illusion. Illusion is a dream. A dream is a playground of beliefs waiting to be seen for what they truly are. Where you "came from" is your only reality, even now. You are the single Breath that knows it is free. Do not look for your-self in the human breath. See that you are the Mind that creates no illusions and is without the need of a door to be found.

Come, I will show you. ❖ ❖

THE NURSERY'S RHYME

❖ ❖ ❖

Let's begin by acknowledging the many tears you shed over the "loss" of your Soul.

It is time to dry them.

Now place yourself in the Nursery where the soft petals of Reality fill the room with the fragrance of what is true. This is *your* room in Timelessness. It is where you live the awareness of being. It is where you are the Moment—Infinity in a single breath.

In making this Reality *your Self* . . . you create a human world that becomes a sane world. And a sane world is a kind world. ❖ ❖

YOU ARE THE QUIETNESS

 You will find a Treasure in this book that you write from your honesty. It has been placed there by your Wish to remember who you are. Take this time away from Time and be forgiving of all that is forced and illusory.

Delight in the sweet solitude of your own thoughts, of your own rich mind which contains only Love within it. Welcome true perception and be reassured it has never gone away. It is your *unseen* self that brings all meaning.

How lovely it is to encounter the divine Hush amid all the voices calling. . . calling. . . This is the Sound that holds you in happiness. Gathering its softness around you brings deeper riches than can be imagined. In the Deep Silence that you are, the creative void forms worlds upon worlds of Wonder that you lovingly offer to your cherished human experience.

What keeps Murmuring in you, blossoms *as* your human life and all of it is made peaceful and beautiful. ❖ ❖

COME HOME

This moment is *all* of life. It is found in Its deep silence and nurturing invisibleness. It is a Presence deeper than the space you stand in; richer than the sounds beyond it; closer than the you that moves on little feet. This moment is the Changeless that is more true and real than what you have come to trust and believe is solid. It is what gives the "solid" meaning and goodness.

You think that what is Real is not real because you are no longer aware of Heart as substance. You are Heart and only that. As you look to the sights and sounds of a tangible world dreaming itself up you cannot find yourself for you are not tangible.

It was in the childhood days that the temporal replaced the everlasting. You compliantly took on the name given to you to please and to be included. You thought you had to and suddenly, people became "authorities." You suspected you had betrayed yourself. Everything was wrong now because you didn't have yourself anymore. You never wanted to lose sight of the Being you really are. But you believe you have and you can't find your way back. You think Life is displeased with you. You think a lot of silly things, having put a human face on Life, but then, you know only faces now.

The Candle of your Soul still glows brightly within you, confirmed by the wonders you create. Trust your creations, they remind you of your Sacred Name and assure you *Forever and Everything* is calling you that, too.

 Come Home—to yourself. You're already there in your Heart. ❖ ❖

THE CANDLE YOU LEFT BEHIND

I will tell you today about a small unlit candle you left behind in a hidden corner of the Garden that you now visit too infrequently. It is the Garden of Eternity that has gone into shadow because you have become distracted by the bright bugle sounds that fill your current world.

When you lived in that Garden the little candle glowed from within you, giving you its light, its warmth, and its guidance. It resided in your heart and you never knew darkness, confusion, or separation.

When you decided to dream about that other world, you thought you could not take the little candle with you, for in that other world light is poised from without in a big lamp that sits in a sky that is blue. When the lamp goes away the blue sky grows dark and very deep. And when it is dark, tiny specks of light appear that wink at you and seem to say unknowable things that stir your mind to memories you cannot remember. You call out to them but think them too far to hear, and then you wonder:

"Oh, what spell can I be under to think myself in a world so set apart? What is this dream that has me beguiled and missing the little candle that so patiently waits to light my heart, my world, once more?"

And this, alone, is your unhappiness—to no longer feel the Nearness that never leaves you. We of the Heavens, hear you. ❖ ❖

UNDERSTANDING WHAT HAPPENED

❖ ❖ ❖

 How did the bad dream begin? Where did the happiness go? The answer is simple: as you turned your focus on an outer existence, its world appeared to "come at you" *logically*. You perceived an orderly collection of vibrant images containing intelligence, cause, and history. How could you disagree with such a coherent and all-encompassing point of view? Being empathetic, you didn't feel you could be contrary to so much certainty.

To not clash with this tide of perception which denied the existence of the inner life and felt more insistent than your intuitive wisdom, you simply put away what you could not share or make useful. Now you were neither in the world nor in yourself. You were nowhere.

You chose not to fight the criticism aimed at you; it was the pervasive way of this place. It seemed more peaceful to be in the wrong, so you (unconsciously) turned yourself into a properly flawed human in need of constant humanizing. This activity, which fit with the notions of the time and the culture, had the added benefit of keeping you nicely "employed" and distracted from the real question at hand whose answer seemed forbidden to you. Your creativity was put to perpetual self-improvement.

Wanting to hide your incomprehension, you made yourself solitary in a culture of extroverts. Because you love people, this felt like failure— *your* failure, *your* insufficiency. But is it not understandable that you should have come to feel unsure of yourself while walking in a dream that caused you to deny your subtle but most deeply felt knowing? Your isolation was a sound choice; it kept you internally intact until you could find your way to reclaiming yourself.

Be kind to your human, she is innocent. She is still the gentle little girl you became in order to walk the sleeping world and fulfill a journey of awakening and resolution—a journey to affirm your Truth of Being while caught in a dream about what is not so. There are others like you in similar bewilderment, not knowing what to call it. Share with them your experience, they will be comforted.

But, no longer seek understanding from those who do not feel this bewilderment. You have been giving them undeserved authority. ❖ ❖

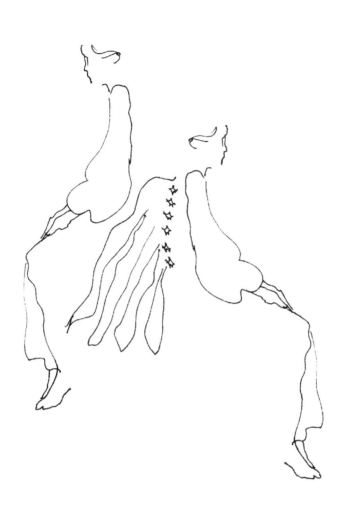

THE "THERE" THAT NEVER WENT AWAY

❖ ❖ ❖

You miss the uncomplicated Reality.

You miss it so that you will not forget it as you turn away from your own true desires. In your willingness to empathize with those of your current world-view, you take on feelings, perceptions, and sensibilities that are not your own. You have silenced your own feeling self. In order to adjust to the dream reality you have engaged all of your attention to what is around you and not within you. You remember deciding to do this early on.

You worked so hard at it. You thought sincerely it was the thing to do, and your belief has been the worm in the apple of your human life. It is this single concept that has given rise to the unbearable loss of self.

You can calmly stand apart from a surface world of others who are indifferent to the way of inner things. Everyone exists in the internal reality—you need not worry about them. It was your loving nature and fragile position as a little child that made you think that you had to be concerned for them and alter yourself to reach them.

You can confidently face a surface world of people doing things incomprehensible to you and generating different experiences from your own. Do not feel you must join them or even agree; you need not even care what they believe or do. Instead, turn inward and go to yourself with gladness, you contain all that you love and all that you think is missing. This is not being selfish, this is what is needed. In this detachment, you abandon no one; *you* are the one you have abandoned.

Never fear that you can harm another, you are incapable of harming anything. The world is safe from unkindness coming from you. Know this. Give no external your power. *Listen to yourself.* What comes from you is full with Life. In your perception of reality, only you matter, you cannot live through another person. You have been "nice" too long. Believe in yourself and your understanding. Cease compromising what you know. You can risk being thought wrong by a world that dozes. ❖ ❖

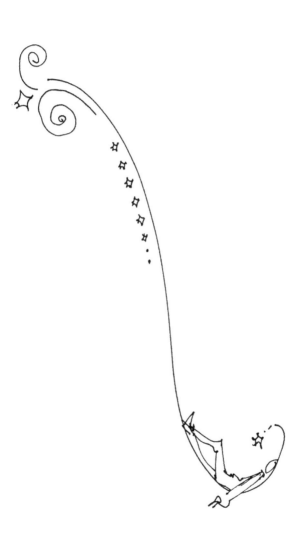

THE WHISPER OF A WING IN FLIGHT

❖ ❖ ❖

It is your nature to receive knowledge for living from your Inner Being.

No one can speak the words of wisdom you want to hear. All True Wisdom originates within the self. Draw this wisdom from yourself. Believe it lives in you. Express yourself to yourself. All Eternity will hear. You are all of Eternity.

A cluttered mind cannot feel empowered. Freedom is found in self-expression with no concern for outcome. Be simple. What is lasting is the substance of the Self perpetually creating, giving forth. What is pure and true and of the greatest value is the self believing in the Self and the abundance within. The world will never understand. It isn't meant to. The world and its approval is not the purpose of life.

You entered this dream of seeming external approval merely to strengthen the power and the resolve to be yourself in a world of illusion. You can succeed in this now by reclaiming your nature.

Look for yourself no longer in the world but let yourself be carried forward by the invisible Wings that have been quietly carrying your Strength and Resolve. ❖ ❖

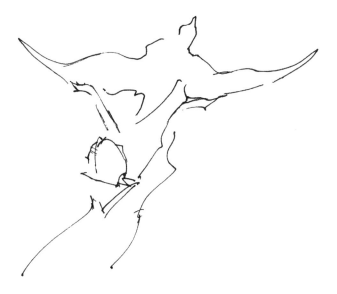

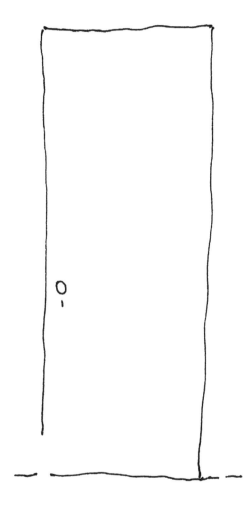

TWO

YOU WILL HEAR ONLY GOODNESS

❖ ❖ ❖

You bring doubt to this dialogue with yourself. You expect to find the disapproval and censure you hear in the world. But as you persist in turning to your inner Whisper, the trust in what you are will return to you. It is your relationship with what is *within* that matters. This is the foundation of all other connections. Your world will reflect and become filled with an ease and an order that surpasses all things of outer perception. There is so much happiness to be derived from letting go of the voice of the outer world.

Stand among the Stars that fill your Higher Self. Let Wisdom's breath remove the doubts that churn within you as you behold the little Suns that spin the thread of your immortal Life. Here, swept up by the brilliance of your Higher Being, Inspired Ideas will become your thoughts. Here, Faith will resume its reign and sweep away all need for consolation.

You are a self so sweet, so sure, so complete— nothing is needed to make life happen or work. Life is unfolding from an uninterrupted flow of *good*. It is this Good that you are. You are what IS and only this. Rest in this knowledge and let the noise of the world dim to your awareness.

You will then hear only Love and it will become the world. ❖ ❖

SUCH A SWEET PLAYFULNESS

❖ ❖ ❖

Oh, how you trouble yourself over your Soul's "unavailability." You struggle to find yourself in an illusion of disconnectedness.

But the way to yourself is the one of quiet peace and trust. Lay aside all concepts of what to do and how to be. Bask in the untroubled Moment that is unconcerned with what was or will be. When you find the inner world, the outer one will comply.

You are not the unhappy child of your imagining. You are not the confused self of your feelings. You are not what you have come to think you are. You are a Being of simplicity in an infinite sky of possibilities that unfolds to reveal what is always present. Each instant holds Everything in its giving Hands which, you, the Beloved, are designed to receive. Your part is sweet—it has all been done for you. You are a bringer of Gifts and it is Magnificent Life that is being given.

In trusting this inner Presence as the reality of yourself you will find your world abundant, your mind at peace, and your heart full with joy.

There will be Magic to share. ❖ ❖

PRAYER

While in the dream you will not encounter your Eternalness in the halls of pomp and circumstance. No Truth is brought forth from a string of ornamental words. What is true appears only when you *know* you are whole.

It is singular your connection to life, but your human mind sees division and cannot allow what is unlike itself. You have let your human mind redefine your uninterrupted silent communication with your Eternalness and made it merely audible prayer. To your human mind, prayer is a thing required to correct loss and separation.

A sense of loss has taken over your better judgment. Tangled thinking distracts you from the pain of this loss and disorganizes your hopes and undermines your trust in the possible. It is through this prism that you look for your Self with a clouded inward gaze. Is it any wonder that you cannot find or feel or know the Meaningful Dialogue you have with Life? You mistrust yourself.

Is it any wonder you are confused by the mornings that keep coming with a fresh collection of old rituals and new obligations in a world drawing you ever outward and away from yourself? You willingly go down this programmed path wanting to be welcomed into the community of humans which is now the "only game in town." Your simple free nature has become an external concept and you've become obedient to something *outside yourself*. In all of this, of course, you have found a need to plead for help. Prayer, the constant true communication with who you are, has become lost to desperation.

But, come, *tell yourself who you are*. We will call

this, Prayer. All that is needed is to listen for the Word beyond words and let It speak in you. Pray by telling yourself of Oneness and how deeply beloved you are in Infinity. This releases the never-ending Word to become your own.

The bond that has not broken can dominate the morning and fill the day with a confidence that will not be tinged with doubt and fear.

So simple is the divine language . . . and your nature. The Word of Spirit is a living thing, a life-giving thing. Let yourself receive It. Let it speak in you. When you utter the assurance of what already is, you give yourself your Life. You create your life. You create your world. Let this be Prayer. ❖ ❖

YOUR ROOM AT HOME

❖ ❖ ❖

Lost in an illusion of believing that it is unfair to remember what others do not recall, you prevent yourself from finding your place in the world. You love your earthly world and all its people but you let few know  it. You think them disapproving that you do not join in the consensus. You dare not be different. You think being different separates you. But it is the fear of self-expression that separates you from yourself and your sense of life. It is time to stand again in Timelessness and fulfill your human wish from here. Come find your Eternal Self.

There is a Room, not quite a room as you know one now. One filled with a Love so unlike the love talked about in the outer feeling world. This eternal place is *your* Room—the one that has kept Itself warmly wrapped around you. The one you never left though you closed your eyes and thought you stood far away in a shadow of confusion. It was only the littlest belief that had a hold of you, a belief *that you must forget what is real.* Gently now, allow yourself to remember. It is not forgotten in you. You *know who you are.* You know and have the right to remember. You can do all the things that are true of Life, you are Its expression. You can be again what you have never stopped being. You are everything you are, and nothing you are not.

You have not acquired a separated self that needs coddling and comforting—you are not a body. You can never go where life does not live or become what Life is not. That is a cosmic impossibility. It is funny that you think you can. But then, you think many funny things that do not serve you well or bring you the happiness that it is your true nature to feel.

You like it here in your Room, don't you? It is safe and warm, with your Heart's belongings all around, always ready to have you come and play. There are no rules or Rulers here. No need to search above the clouds for answers. No impatient waiting for tomorrows. Existence unfolds on its own to reveal what has always been, even if you've never seen it in that incarnation before.

It is playful this Life that keeps changing coats and slippers to appear now one thing and then another, and then all over again but, differently. You get caught up in the *differentness* and think it is somehow significant. But it isn't. It's always just Infinity as you, playing, being creative in a Room that is unchanging, but never the same.

Can you see that you are standing in it, right now? ❖ ❖

MEET YOUR ETERNAL SELF

A gift of Warmth inhabits you. It presents itself to you not only on wintery mornings when the fire has yet to be lit in the hearth of your outer room.

You are the recipient of the Wisdom designed to envelop you with the Self of yourself that you cannot see in the world around you. You are upheld within Promises that never needed to be made and never waited for. Why promise what has been given? Why wait for what is already here? All Beings are filled to capacity and running over. Hopes come fully realized.

Are you aware of the little feet tiptoeing into your room, small and sweet and unshod? They make no noise, they leave no trace. They come to remind you that you, too, are made of quietness, of a "nearly not there reality" that hums throughout the Soul of one who *is* and always *will be* . . . *infinite*.

You can tell you are in repose as you write this—you are perceiving something kind. A great softness overcomes you, smoothing out tight corners, elevating thoughts, breathing out furies derived from misinformed conclusions about a world that seems to be what it is not. You are safe within yourself.

Now, see how wonderfully free you are—you are Life. ❖ ❖

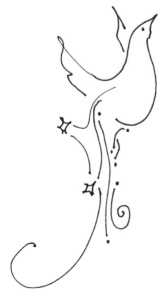

A MERE DREAM

❖ ❖ ❖

You entered and engaged with a material world only to find that you had to hide your knowing. The veil fell upon you as with all others, but you made a vow to keep memory alive for reasons you don't remember.

In your willingness to put aside your deeper nature, you broke the bonds of trust with yourself and the Infinite within you—it is a betrayal and you are disappointed in yourself. Now you believe you've lost your power and are trapped. You experience confusion only because your loss of

Spirit feels like the withdrawal of Life itself—the deepest loss imaginable. Every loss is based on this original one.

Choosing the human experience is not an offence against what is Real. It is only dreaming a dream, and none of it is really happening the way it appears to be happening. Within the dream is the power to know you are dreaming.

And why are you dreaming up this human world?

To forever break the spell of your own deep-seated attachment to being a human dreamer, you came to dream a dream that has no other purpose of its own.

Consciously understanding that you are dreaming while you are dreaming is the start of freedom. Take heart. You are successfully rethinking a very convincing illusion. ❖ ❖

HERE IN THIS MOMENT IS ONLY JOY

Here in this Moment life is present. Joyful Life, bestowing an ordered mind contained in tranquil emotions from which to express yourself. Here in this Moment where nothing Everlasting can be seen or heard or felt by touch—*all* is yours to know and to experience.

Yes, even while you dream of a temporary kind of world, this precious Moment with all Eternity within it is where you remain. Go to yourself, knowing Who is there, and draw from yourself with confidence. Drink from the inner Spring of Life. Trust the words that you dare to utter to yourself away from the noise of the world outside. Trust yourself, let your knowing glow through the unreal darkness you have made real out of politeness.

Do not be afraid to believe. You will not be betrayed. Hardship was a belief that could be healed and you bravely dealt with it. It is behind you now; don't look back. The day has been renewed. Rely on your inner knowing, your inner constancy. *You can be at home in your own mind.*

Trust yourself in this Moment. ❖ ❖

IN A VERY QUIET CORNER

 There lives an Inaudible Presence in a corner of your room. It lives there night and day. The other parts of the house are perfectly ordinary. You move around in them and get the usual things done while the days flow into nights and round and round you go.

But, there, in that quietest corner is the deep Understanding that came with you into this human world. It keeps itself available but unobtrusive while the busy human world conspicuously tends to the "truly necessary" things for life.

Oh, do listen to what has no sound in your very quiet corner, it is where lives the *Intuition that tells you of your wholeness and keeps you in it.* ❖ ❖

IT SLIPS THROUGH

While you nap in a concrete world there lives a reverie inside your head about another Place, another Way. The reality of Home never leaves you. At times you allow the inner Landscape that glows unnoticed through your dreaming to fill the shadowed corners of your human life. It is *then* that the sparkling rivulets of raindrops swirling on your windowpane are recognized to be the Beauty that is within all things.

This glimpse of inner Splendor drapes its coverlet of truth over illusion to show you what has *always been there. For nothing else exists.* ❖ ❖

THE PROBLEM WITH SINCERE FEELINGS

You know that you dream at present of what is *not quite true*. All around you others dream, too, unaware that they are asleep to the greater reality. In the reverie you share you hear them loudly clamor their Convictions and Attitudes as they play out their human role with attitude and conviction. Their unconflicted earnestness is the single quality that draws you in and holds you captive to the human drama. You know that life is a *feeling* thing, incalculably subtle and more present than all the forms about it. But you are fooled now.

You are drawn into error by confusing the *human emotions* with the *feeling nature* of Reality. In this lifetime you have willingly relinquished your own wisdom to align with the dearest faces, the warmest hearts that live in a massive delusion.

You are full of caring for your fellow travelers but you wonder how can you love others and remain true to yourself in this big world of people and all their sincere feelings. Is it kind to be indifferent to the human theatre of high emotion? You have forgotten to believe in, and affirm, the Sovereign Being that you are as you stand in a dream with other Sovereign Beings who are thinking they "need to be loved." To realize this is the reason you came.

Devotion to your true self will fill the void caused by your gaze on a world merely spinning a dream of needy people. Bring home your gaze and let that world go merrily spinning along. You entered this trance only to see *yourself* rightly. ❖ ❖

A TRUTH SO SIMPLE

How well you have learned to worry about keeping yourself safe. Worry is a way of *doing something*. Doing nothing is nothing you understand. Life has become effort. You no longer trust the quiet moment where no thought occurs, where you just feel peaceful *for no reason at all*. Yet, be assured, in that moment you will find the problem gone.

It is not in acquired knowledge that the infinite good is brought forth. Life is closer than that. You keep relying too much on human conditioned thinking. You form assumptions by looking at an *externally-driven* picture show that tells you nothing of the everlasting. You become despondent within a mind dependent on mere impressions.

All that is needed is a glance inward. What is

waiting there is more real and true than the outer appearances. What is waiting there . . . is your knowing. Believe you are made of unlimited knowing. This is how your unhappiness will find its peace and your questions their answers.

You are the one who walks in a dream—a dream offering only symbols of what is real and possible. Nevertheless, beyond the quirky appearance of each instant is the *Peace* that transforms the illusion. Imagine yourself filled with this peace, and a very kind world will await you. ❖ ❖

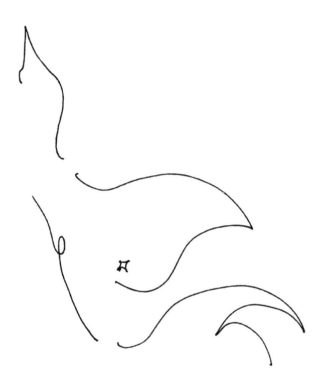

THE MIRACLE OF SIMPLE TRUST

Once upon a Timelessness, you knew the gentlest Gentleness, and it was your own Being.

You feel that it has been replaced by a countenance that no longer feels kind or true to you. You despair that you are without the wisdom and grace that once guided and showed you the way. You can no longer perceive your true nature's serenity in a world enthralled by aggression which you seem to have acquired.

Still, you know in the clarity of the saved memory kept alive by you, that the still small voice, poorly understood, unacknowledged in your world, is the eternal Presence acting within you even now. It does not need to be asked, but waits to be relied upon by your confident expectation.

The day has dawned when you want the True One you are to be restored to you fully. How else can it be returned than by your desire, your permission? To claim its presence is to ask rightly. The thing wanted is already here.

This reality is not too good to be true. You have only forgotten how to feel its presence, and this is not of lasting concern. There is nothing that belongs to you that the Inner One cannot restore. Nothing.

There is a Power overseeing and undergirding your journey through the dream of external existence. It never looks away, never is remote, never becomes diminished by your (temporary) indifference to your Soul and its wisdom.

You are that Power. You are Its means for being. Never mind how it all got lost for you. Never mind what others do, think, or believe. A benevolent goodness is at hand, underfoot, all around and within, bringing order, balance and beauty to human life. The Breath of Life is flowing through illusory worlds, safely keeping dreamers in eternal reality.

Know this, believe this, rely on this invisible inner life. It is the one never truthfully portrayed by your temporal world.

And that, too, is of no concern. ❖ ❖

ALL ARE ONE

❖ ❖ ❖

Your Eternal Beginning is standing with
you here in the Now, bringing Light into
your dream of separation. See how complete you
are, nesting sweetly in this Instant that makes all
instances of "apartness" disappear.

How long you have sought this assurance. How
long you have thought you must look only to a
world of hollow beliefs and demands. How long
you have thought you must uphold your neigh-
bor's choices, forgoing your own better judgment.
Your freedom seemed denied you in the attempt
to play, too earnestly, the game of joining with
others; of loving others before yourself.

You thought joining was love. As you have done
it, it was otherwise. There is no need to force joining to what is not separate. You see bodies. Too

many. You perceive pain. Too much. Feeling your joyful internal self gone, you believe you must loyally join with all pain and share in its burden.

But there is only one of you. *Each* breathes the singular Breath of Substance. *Each* is the presence of the Goodness that begins and fulfills what remains held in Joy.

Each is the Face of Love.

Always, forever, and most wonderfully—when you are giving fully to *yourself*—all receive. ❖ ❖

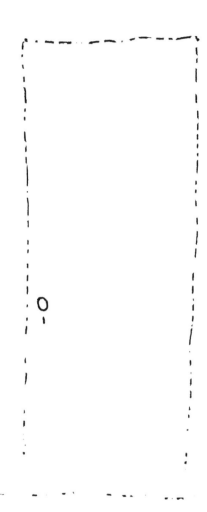

THREE

❖ ❖ ❖

You feel empty. You feel human and controlled by something other than yourself. Yet something in you keeps hoping, *"One day, I will create this,"* and *"One day, I will create that,"* only to find yourself sitting and staring at the blank page. You are waiting to feel inspired. What is missing?

What you are really waiting for is your right relationship with Reality. You make yourself anxious by always needing to acquire something from the *world*. Be it knowledge, approval, permission, or passage of time, you wait, you hope, you try to seduce, you contrive, you dance to another's tune. Where, in all this, is the freedom and inner space to create the wonders that quietly live within you?

Truth is not found in the world of other people but it shows its Presence there. Speak with your pen and paper unconcerned with how it will be received. You care too much about pleasing others. Vibrating within you is an ever-present exhilaration that fills your mind with wonder. Result is not purpose; expression is Life lived.

You are not of the world, so what does the world matter? It matters that you be with yourself in good companionship—without judgment, ambition, or competitiveness. From people, you need no understanding, no inclusion, no recognition. *Be what you are. Be* invisible. *Be* eternal. *Be* star-filled. Make your inner Self the one most real of all and, magically, your human world will become something of value.

Now take your pen and exclaim all the way to the Stars that Happiness is the cause and purpose of the creative Soul forever and always! Happiness is the only Life there is. ❖ ❖

THE FEAR OF "GOD"

You make too much of the world of being human. You are not human. You are all that is Life, ever whole and unchangeable. Be still. In the Quiet you will hear all you need to know. Listen with *trust* and the Silence will heal confusion.

Ah, but there is a problem. You are surrounded with judgments that Spirit, the one called "God," is a severe critic of your behavior and frowns upon your very nature. Now you think you must be good, for you are not that now. You are living in belief systems that say you must obey many rules and practices and perhaps even wait many lifetimes to slay your flawed "original" nature. You are aware these are not *your* thoughts, but you act as if you must consider them or appear insensitive and rude. And so by being so well-mannered, you have become enmeshed.

Now you, too, have made Spirit *personality* and you are confused by this delusion. You fear the outer world, believing that you must give it much consideration, and you fear the inner world, which you think is lost to you. That is why you cannot turn to your inner self and receive the unconventional wisdom living there, waiting to guide you. You go into the world and are drawn into what clutters your emotions and disturbs your peace of mind.

You must understand how easily ideas and beliefs that are not yours take hold of you. It is the nature of your world that thoughts attach to the unaware. Error does not come *from* you. It is the unconscious flotsam of a meaningless thought-field hovering about, incessantly kept alive from being trapped in remembered time. It floats by ready to be identified with—or dissolved by having its lie made consciously known. Your agreeing to join with the world has been a "sticky" proposition

Nevertheless, your inner Wisdom can reach through the notions that have attached to you and set you free from them. Live for yourself.

There is no world to resist, condemn, or analyze. But there is a need to stand firm and stay fully conscious of a Self not made of human matter. ❖ ❖

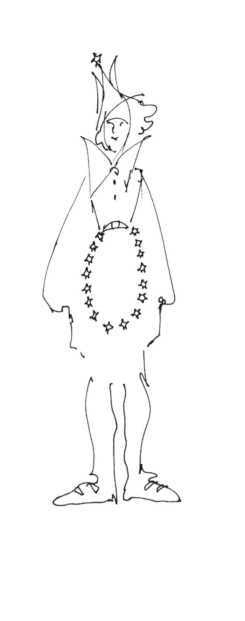

POWER

❖ ❖ ❖

You were made whole before Time began. The Light of the Universal Mind is gleaming as your mind and coursing through your veins to illuminate the morning sun. You are empowered.

You have the world at your feet though you relentlessly peer through shop windows at what you do not have. In your forgetting, you pray for a magic formula to give you courage and faith while standing in a Life that undergirds, sustains, guides, and nurtures. All knowing is yours; know *yourself*. What has been hidden to you will be made evident.

You need not search for what has been given. You need only express it with joy and self-assurance. You are the possessor of fulfillment.

Yours is hallowed ground, with a crown of softly braided assurances that hold your power intact. Your power is such that there is nothing to learn, nothing to earn, nothing to wait for. A small turn of mind, a daring willingness, a fanning of the flame of faith will set you free. All power is yours. All Life, all possibilities, *are at hand*. You confirm the Good.

Act from *believing*. Trust, and let go the world's opinions on these matters. ❖ ❖

SMALL, PATIENT STEPS

❖ ❖ ❖

 Mornings are an invention of a mind thinking itself in Time; hear the *infinite* whisper to you this "morning." Because you dream you are finite, you cannot accept the reality of unlimited being. However, even in a dream Spirit creates what is true. It knows nothing of lack.

Use your imagination to conceive of the true nature of things. Bring patience and humility to your journey to Awakening. Small steps will avoid resistance, and perseverance will build confidence. In the obscured dimension of Time and Space lives the Truth that cannot disappear. You have never ceased looking for It because It is Who you are.

One "day," one "morning, Eternity will wear your

name. In this manner will the face of Love be yours. You will no longer be merely wishing for your true self.

Do not wait for this day. Do not look for it. It reveals Itself when you no longer think in terms of *wanting it*. How can you want what you have? Merely suffer it not be visible for now. Fill your day with confident activity and life-affirming faith. All will be done for you as you place your being into serene trust and unconcern.

What you seek is already yours and will come into view when you no longer seek it. ❖ ❖

KNOWING WITHOUT WORDS

❖ ❖ ❖

The Infinite is present without the need for human conversation.

You are often tired of verbal exchanges with others, aren't you? You are tired of human word-thoughts and the noise they make and the energy they take from you. They go round and round like a wheel that has forgotten why it turns. But it cannot stop.

To you, who recall the easy knowing that is instantaneous and clear, your mind has become a disheartening place of literalness. To you, rendering knowledge into bits of shape and structure and sound, inhibits flow of expression. And you have become disheveled from reducing yourself caring about manufactured cold facts.

You needn't have concern about all this. Do not resist this temporary way of doing things. Remain loyal to yourself and remember that the Heart of life is nearer than any words about it. It is only illusion that wants you to use one little utterance after another.

Human storytelling takes on a fulfilling meaning when you know all minds are One and nothing need be conveyed. All is known by all. You cannot *tell* the truth, only can you *know* and *be* it for yourself. Life is not artificial and its rewards are not found in consensus. ❖ ❖

A SINGLE VOICE

You have never displaced yourself from the heart of Love.

Spiritual wholeness knows nothing of your concerns about not staying true to your nature; you are in Oneness eternally. There is no *return* journey for one who never left.

Yet there you sit in a dialogue with your innerness, writing words that would indicate, by virtue of their external existence, a kind of separation. But you are now and always infinite, a radiant sphere of Light within a Radiant Sphere of Light. *Your dialogue is from a single voice.*

It is your present inventive nature that uses the "English" language to make the Ineffable available to you. You stand in your manifested reality and receive and weave into *words* what your subtle heart "says." This is so with each and every manifestation in your world—the inner essence ever becoming symbol, ever changing form. Let it change—the *essence* is the never-ending Presence. Rely solely on essence, you will know comforting reasonableness. Think confidently, letting life blossom from within you to show your life.

Each objectified human moment is the deep Reality showing through but *needing to be understood rightly.* Hear the single voice of life. It is your own and no other. ❖ ❖

A SACRED CHOICE

You come at your life as if you need to *fix it and yourself*. Everything is on hold until it all gets fixed, and of course, you only find ever more things to fix.

And yet, and yet . . .

The truth is that you rise with your morning sun having emerged childlike from Infinity. You think that you sleep at night, to find rest from the world. But you *sleep*, in order to *wake up from the world* and give yourself a long drink of pure Life in the encounter with your inner Self.

In wanting to trust in your wholeness, is it possible, that you are already, "perfectly fixed?" And can you allow yourself to be innocent in a world that tells you you are merely human and deeply flawed? It is this sacred choice to be making. ❖ ❖

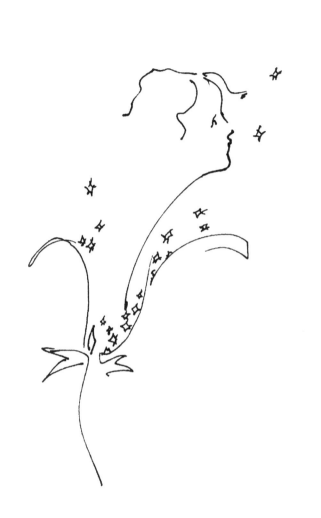

YOU HAVE DONE NO WRONG

❖ ❖ ❖

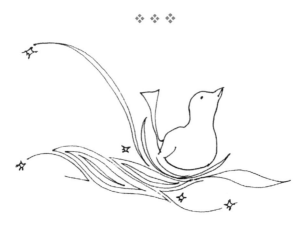

Your True Nature is the one that breathes beyond the human one.

There is no need for you to go on believing in the deception that you are merely a body encased in Space and Time. This conviction has caused you to weave yourself into a disconnected being in a world made from artificial threads.

You have become afraid. You are confused by all your human ways. You are worried about the Anger and think you must control it lest it destroy you and all the tender wonders within you. You have feared that it has taken away your gentle innocence. But the Thing Within is *indestructible* and cannot ever be harmed. Your human emotions cannot separate you from Reality. Condemning yourself by trying to control them merely restricts your expression. Let them be the signposts to your authenticity. Do not judge what is only energy.

Listen carefully: you are not the human story. In believing you are, you attempt to have power over a self that is not who you are. You have abandoned the real life by focusing too much on the external and trying to overcome it. As you let go, as you slowly give the outer world less and less consideration by not concerning yourself with getting it right, the you that is of Forever will flourish. Give no important attention to the thing you create *out there*. It does not tell you who you are. You are eternal and complete and limitless. You are kind and good and full of joy.

Be this most happy self and Life will hold you in Its loving arms. ❖ ❖

YOU WERE NEVER LOST

Do you hear your own breath in the swaying meadow grasses that line your day as you stroll through your city streets? Do you hear the whispering Trees that lean toward you in friendship and tell you of the Life you share?

Yes, you do, and you know that in your dream world it is a rare occurrence to sense this "familial" connectedness to all the beings in All That Is. You are the one who delights in your bit of fair Earth where you walk the narrow Path of your Soul, which has remained in Oneness. ❖ ❖

POETRY IN MOTION

❖ ❖ ❖

There are ripples in your night sky that look like indigo silk being pulled over the stars. This is your thinking as it floats through Timelessness to create a new world.

You are an Eternal Being creating in a silent Present Moment. Everywhere you go there is a world confirming your infinite nature. You are the Spark in the firefly's wing and the Light cast by the Moon on the footpath it illuminates. You are the Rays of the Sun awakening the hills of climbing Morning Glory to glorify each morning.

You are strong with gentleness and wise with joy. You are a fool for tender things. You are more than your world can see and more than you remember. You are so much and all that is plain. You are

the promise made by the Love that animates only
. . . everything.

You are the simplicity of placing one tiny foot in front of the other on the way of brightly-lit stones. Twinkling EarthStars in an *inverted* sky are your journey's topography for you are the traveler who never leaves Home, but pretends doing so. ❖ ❖

FOUR

NO WANTING

You turn and reach into your Heart. You are embraced. All is made right. You have suffered from thinking what is not true. The need to achieve an end is the only thing standing in your way. You distance yourself in a mind that *wants*.

You are within Infinity—as It is, so are you. For the inner to become your awareness, release your focus on wanting the outer to be other than it appears to be. It is effect, you are cause.

Know what is here though it is invisible, and duality will dissolve. *Trust* and do not concern yourself with how loss of trust came to be. You are empowered to set illusion free from its hold on you.

You are the Invisible ever becoming. See what you ever become. ❖ ❖

THERE IS JOY IN DUALITY

There is a Wish waiting on a faraway star that you placed there for not believing it was yours to own. This is the source of your troubles. You have come to examine each moment and turn life into a thing incompatible with simple faith. You *are* Faith but now you *look* and *analyze* and *weigh* and *measure* and want *guarantees* that remove you from your sense of completeness.

Can you show to illusory shadows the Light within? The infinite Light exists because *you know it does*. Recognize the gift of your unprovable knowing that is contained in a Mind that knows all there is to know. Give to yourself the full measure of the Truth that is unacknowledged in the marketplace. No one need agree with you. Agree with yourself.

Adapt a carelessness to your gait and stride into wide open spaces with confidence and with no map. Your map resides in your Soul and is ever a part of you and ever present to enable you a journey true and lighthearted. You try too hard to make the world measure up to the simple ways of Spirit. Live in the world with acceptance not resignation, there is much that delights you when you are true to yourself. See your being untrammeled by conformity.

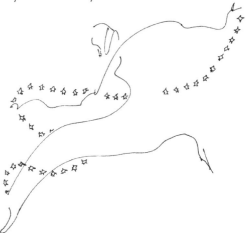

You are a dancer of Light. There is joy to be found even in *duality* when you dance to your own sweet music. Some will join in. ❖ ❖

MAGICAL WORLD

❖ ❖ ❖

You are the one who sees the Deep Moon brush its Light over your big concrete city. Its glow makes the man-made structures look like Trees decked for celebration.

You see magic everywhere from a Heart that never leaves Reality. Standing in your sea of humanity, is the Infinite Child you are. You have a Boat and the promise of a Map that rewrites itself to the needs of the moment. You have a Captain who never tires and knows the way through uncharted waters for He is the waters and the lands within them. You are surrounded by a world that is created by the beneficent Presence that is your Soul.

Your Soul—the most joyful place to be—is where no adjustment to life is ever necessary, where all effort has been laid to rest and all work has been done. Your Soul is your clarity within the twinkling night-sky holding the unknown but not unknowable.

There is no room for doubt. The Wings that hold you aloft make you supple in movement and sure-footed and free. You are this and much, much more for you *know* Life loves you.

And you love life, even in its incarnations made of concrete. ❖ ❖

IN YOUR LITTLE HOUSE

There is a little stair in your home that reaches to the Stars. It leads to the house where you live in Eternity. You cannot see it with your eyes, and you don't know it's there until you stop looking at the outer world.

You visit each night when your human sleeps. You love being back among your little possessions that don't possess you. Here, where you are at peace you know a deep contentment, for all around you is the assurance of only Love and Acceptance.

You have always thought it odd that to be human is to forgo the vastness that is perfect joy. But it is always with you, this Joy and this Vastness, even in the human that you are dreaming of being, for she is only a sleeper reaching to stir to the Life that cannot be renounced. ❖ ❖

YOUR DANCING SHOES AWAIT YOU

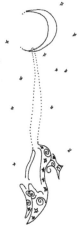

Seriousness has become the order of your day for you do not dance to the music your Heart is making. Yet, placed in a secret corner of your mind, patiently waiting, are life's Dancing Shoes—shoes that belong to the lighthearted creature you are. Not to dance this Dance has caused your despair—your world is cumbersome for not believing that Joy is all there is.

You wonder how it could be that you have lost so much of yourself. And you wonder how you can be so spellbound to a world in turmoil. But you have simply come to believe you require a *body* to dance. How at odds you are with this false embodiment you have made your identity.

It is from this heaviness of thought that you look soulfully to the butterfly who flutters gracefully through your world and who is, in fact, there to remind you of your own true nature.

To be acknowledged by the world, you have sacrificed your Self, have closed your Wings and put away your Dancing Shoes. This need not be. Dare to cease making the body your being. In relinquishing this deception, Freedom will come and life will be a delight once more—all a mere thought away. The Inner Self is the Melody and you are its Dancer. ❖ ❖

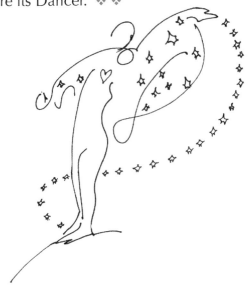

YOUR OTHER WORLD

❖ ❖ ❖

 In a sheltered corner of your inner House is a friendly little Chair that *created itself just for you*. Warm and soft with rounded corners, it is perfect for rest and relaxation. It doesn't ever desire to be anything other than what it is, and it is proud to offer itself to you and to your needs throughout Forever. It was born for the times that cause pauses in your livingness.

You treasure the little Chair that lives ever in wait of your visit Home. You love this Chair that holds all Hopes and keeps all Dreams from growing weary. And you love *yourself* when sitting in that Chair, knowing that it patiently kept itself for your return while you spent time visiting that most eccentric of spinning planets. The two of you howl with laughter and are filled with bewilderment at the kinds of tales you tell of it—neither one of you can quite believe any of these goings on.

No, you are never alone in your Other World. There you find the company of many Friendlinesses of the kind that are simply not believable to those living on that "so smart" spinning planet you visit. ❖ ❖

WHO BRINGS THE DAY

❖ ❖ ❖

Sometimes you are daring. Sometimes you tell yourself the truth. Sometimes you defy the teachings of the dream you're dreaming.

In those times you know it is the radiant Being *you are* that moves the infinite Light over the moon to make the day reappear, and not an impersonal *scientific* principle at work.

Yes, sometimes you see more clearly. Sometimes you feel more rightly. Sometimes the Everlasting shows itself to you in the ordinary. You become peaceful then on your little planet as you nestle at the foot of the loyal tree that only *appears* rooted on an Earth that pulses with reminders of Loving constancy. You rejoice in remembering that life is in reality, a *Poem*. ❖ ❖

YOU ARE THE FRAGRANCE OF THE ROSE

❖ ❖ ❖

The Great Nothing holds only everything in perfect repose. To think creates distance and produces time and space. Thinking is different than knowing. Let your outer mind not attempt to understand life. Trying to understand anything separates you from the reality of it.

There is nothing to understand. Life is complete; it brings all that is needed to each instant. Look to the flowers growing themselves with delicate un-concern—they rely on the unseen Gardener who never shuns the garden's work. Yours is the mind that simply forgot that Reality is lived only from quiet knowing and from no other way.

You are the tenderly held Thing in the everlasting moment. Can you understand the fragrance of the rose? ❖ ❖

TELL YOURSELF THIS HAPPY TRUTH

You are a bright Sacred Circle. Whole. Complete.

In your inner Being lives the ever-unfolding Dawn that il-luminates for you the ways of perfect freedom. It opens each  morning with nothing nothing *nothing* from the past. It closes each night with no idea of tomorrow.

It is *as* you that the Infinite plays its instrument of loving Song. It is *through* you that a life-affirm-ing Garden grows. All Infinite Wonders are urged into being by a soft breath, a plain intention, the smallest gesture. In you is Simplicity's command, free of the shadows of doubt and effort.

Need you speak of this to anyone? No, it is in the telling of this to yourself that the world you now journey in will confirm it. You are the receiver and the giver of the Light that emanates from your *secret silent knowing* of who you are.

This Quietness brings Love into view. ALL life receives what is within. Be restful in this reassuring knowledge. You have been made unbroken. Nothing more need be done.

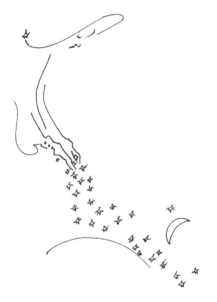

Rejoice in your good and joyful nature and see that the ends of the Earth are being nourished. ❖ ❖

YOU ARE THIS

❖ ❖ ❖

Be still, and you will sense something true. *Be still,* this instant has no other beyond it. This Moment speaks. It speaks to you. Hear what it says.

Within you is the World you think you see no more. You need not reach for it. It is in stillness that it becomes apparent. So much becomes apparent in stillness.

Within you is the Gentleness that is your strength. Within you is the Light that shows the way. Within you are the living words of Love you thought stolen by the Land of Time. You have been standing in a starlit night that closed no door on the Eternal Life.

There is no loss. Nowhere is there a world of jagged edges gaudily painted up and clamoring for your agreement. You live in the perpetual ordinary moment that is just like the one before—new, fresh, innocent and full with possibilities. You are the Aliveness meant to be only *playing* at being human. You are more than the fingers that touch an outer world that feels real but is only brittle driftwood waiting to become dust.

What is everlasting and real is within you and it is saying: *know who you are.* ❖ ❖

INVENT IT ALL

Invent. Life is waiting to be made real to you with Laughter and from Joy. There are talents in your Ship's hold that exist to make your human journey meaningful and bright.

Invent Infinity, and then invent yourself. Go beyond the waiting way of outer perception and trust the honesty of pure *invention* from your Within. Invent your happiness. Invent this dialogue with your Self. Invent Love and Eternal Reality. Invent and bring into being all that you can *see* before you can see it. This is how to create. Within nothingness is what waits to be formed. What is a lie in the outer world is a truth within. This is the power you possess. ❖ ❖

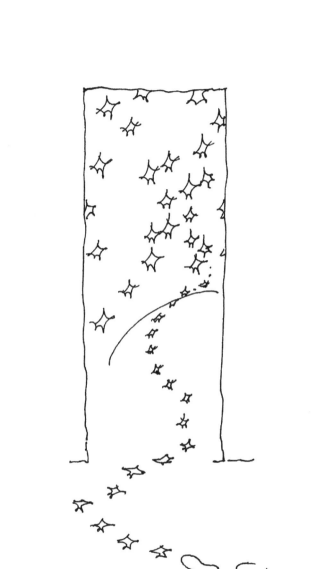

FIVE

CHILD OF THE UNIVERSE

I am a star, said the quiet child, the one pensive and solitaire who grows himself a garden underneath the stair. It was no surprise that the clouds brought him water and the birds seeds from foreign lands. It was no surprise. A big surprise was the tears that kept falling despite the smile on his lips. Tiny crystals flowing down his little round cheeks. One quietly following the other. Every day. Every night.

He was a dear child, full of dreaminess and quiet contemplation. His friends were the flowers and the mice of the field and the butterflies and the other creatures that made their home in his wee garden. He had a wheelbarrow and a watering can. He filled the patches of dryness with sweet earth and watered them with the clean fresh rain the clouds brought him. There wasn't ever a day when he didn't come to his garden and its creatures delighted at the sight of him. He was a soldier of Spirit. A quiet soul who marched to the sound of a hidden rhythm.

He was a child of the Universe. He knew he was a child of the Universe. He listened to the hum of harmony that was within himself. He listened to nothing else. He heard it in others although they didn't hear it in themselves. He was ever vigilant and ever present to the sounds his heart would make, silently passed by the clatter of the day the world would make.

He was quiet in this way. And he was strong. He held to great kindness and when he put up a little fence around his garden it was with love and out of patient understanding. His neighbors were un-aware of the strength of their chatter, the size of their feet and the depth of their unknowing. He found it best to keep to himself and his own out of reach. It had taken him a while to learn this—but when he did, it was with thanksgiving and peace of mind. His heart remained open and his mind willing as he firmly kept his garden gate closed. No one seemed to mind. No one seemed to recognize that the little scrap of land underneath the stair was a lovely garden. And certainly it was too small to care about. Nothing so small and so hidden could mean anything. So they walked by. And so they never knew. ❖ ❖

CPSIA information can be obtained
at www.ICGtesting.com
Printed in the USA
LVHW092251060119
602957LV00001B/51/P

9 780984 881468